An Ordinary Man
With An Extraordinary God

Jimenez Bailey

ISBN-10:
ISBN-13:

Printed In USA

TABLE OF CONTENTS

"The man who views the world at 50, the same as he did at 20, has wasted 30 years of his life."

~Muhammad Ali

DEDICATION

To my parents, James Bailey Sr. and Leilia Bailey-Leahy: Daddy, I understand now what you meant. When you would tell me, "Son, I'm not going to be around forever." Thank you for showing me that your beginning, doesn't have to be your ending; that there is honor in being a good man.

I love you and miss you. I know Heaven is much more beautiful with you in it.

Mother, you have always been my rock; my source of unending love, strength, and inspiration. My love for you is like none other. I can never thank you enough for your unconditional love. You are the most beautiful person in my life, and I will love and protect you until my last breath.

To my brother Benjamin, and sisters Sybil, and Shawndra: Thank you for loving me, when I wasn't always the best brother. One of the things I've learned with God's help, is that we each have a different path to take; that as Family, love is unconditional, and prayer is the glue that holds us together.

To Art Leahy, thank you for being such a wonderful example of how a man should love his wife. You have never wavered in your love and support for Mother, nor us as her children. You are a good man. I love you for the undying love you have for her.

To Pastor Dr. John H. Paxton, who led me to Christ on December 20, 1998. And Pastors Kenny and Brenda Rodgers, who loved me back to Christ in December 2011. You have been, and continue to be, a beacon of God's love and light in my life. I love you.

To Jade, Kemya, Brittany, and Johnathan. There was never a "Step" in my love for you. I'm so proud of the men and women of God that you have become. Continue to seek God with all of your heart.

God has work for you to do!

To Mr. Vincent Harris, Miss Sahnye Styles, and my KPE Media family... Thank you for believing and embracing my vision; for expanding God's Kingdom with a spirit of Godly wisdom and excellence.

To Elder Desireé Harris-Bonner, my spiritual midwife, for helping me birth *"An Ordinary Man with an Extraordinary God".* You were Heaven sent. Thank you for reminding me to breathe and bring my baby to life!

To Erica Michelle, thank you for loving me. Not for what I have, but for who I am in Christ.

FOREWORD

Man of God, in the beginning, God had you on His mind. So much so, that in Genesis 1:27, He decided to create man after His own image; which means, Man was created to be and do great things throughout the world.

You were to rule, reign and have dominion over the fish in the sea and the birds in the sky, over the livestock and all the wild animals, and over all the creatures that moved along the ground; including that ole' (snake), but because of wrong choices made by Adam and Eve, God had to abort His original plan.

However, God couldn't just give up on His creation. He had to go back to the drawing board and create a new plan. There was no way He was going to allow the enemy to win.

What an awesome God we serve!

He loved us so much, that He was willing to wipe the slate clean, and start over with a new "Adam".

God was determined that man would one day take his rightful place, just as He had planned in the beginning... but, it would all come at a cost; the cost of His only begotten Son, Jesus Christ, Who would eventually hang on the cross and serve as a sacrificial offering.

Nevertheless, Jesus understood the part He was required to play, and that it would be bigger than him; yet He would overcome and be victorious, because of the relationship He had with His Father, who resided within Him.

The same applies to you, Man of God.

You can also overcome and be victorious, no matter what you may be facing today. He is waiting for you to surrender your life over to him.

An Ordinary Man with an Extraordinary God was written, so that you would be reminded, that if you allow God to take His 'Extra' and connect it with your 'ordinary', together you can do extraordinary things.

It doesn't matter how many times you've faltered or fallen, He was there to catch you, each and every time.

He wants first place in your life.

That business, that relationship, that money, and those possessions, will never fill you in the way that God desires to fill you. His calling is so much greater than those things, and will never fit inside that small box you have created for yourself, or others have put you in.

It's time to let it GO!

So, will you continue to allow the World's Blueprint for your life to direct your path, or will you respond to the Godly Templates being presented in *An Ordinary Man with an Extraordinary God;* perfectly manifesting His plan, purpose, and vision for your life?

I pray the latter.

Erica Michelle
Author of *"My One Year Sabbatical"*

For I know the plans I have for you, "declares the Lord," plans to prosper and not to harm you, plans to give you hope and a future.

~Jeremiah 29:11

INTRODUCTION

"An Ordinary Man with an Extraordinary God", is a template God has given me to share with those men in the world desiring to live a life submitted and purposed to serving and honoring God.

Even more so, it's the journey of my ups and my downs, my successes, and my failures; the various chapters of my life where I wasn't living for God, but where I was trying to discover what success looked like, while thinking I could attain it by living life the world's way.

Thankfully, with the Lord's help, I eventually found myself on the right path.

Throughout the Bible, we come to understand that the mission of God's men was (and still is) to reveal the plans and purposes of God.

The mandate that God has given us through scripture, extends beyond the chosen people of Israel to the lost. It is to bring others to Christ.

Truly, *"An Ordinary Man with an Extraordinary God"* has been written for the singular purpose of helping men take their rightful place. Not only in the world, but first and foremost, in our homes, leading as husbands and fathers; then, in our communities and churches, as spiritual leaders; and, finally, in our businesses and careers, as marketplace leaders.

In order for this to occur, it is imperative we recognize that Jesus Christ lived and walked this type of life. He was the ultimate Servant Leader.

He is the model we have been given to follow.

One of my favorite stories in the Bible was when Jesus found several men casting nets and He said to them, *"Follow me and I'll make you fishers of men."*

For me, *"An Ordinary Man with Extraordinary God"* is just that, it's the ability for us as men to begin to follow Christ as the lead in our life; in turn, making us capable of becoming fishers of men.

His life provides us with the practical template we need to be in healthy relationships with ourselves, with others, and most importantly, with our heavenly Father; seeking first His Kingdom, knowing then that all the things we have need of will be provided to us.

Not just material things, but ALL things, which includes security, peace, love, joy, stability, etc.

This was a new way of living for me. Throughout my journey of growth and healing, I had gone from having it all, to losing it all. And then one day, I heard him say to me, *"In the past, I let you hold the pen and write the chapters of your life. If you'll let me hold the pen and write, I'll open doors, transform your life, and design something extraordinary!"*

So, when God gave me *"An Ordinary Man with an Extraordinary God"*, people began asking me, "How long has it taken you to write this book?"

I tell them, "53 years".

Each and every chapter that God has written has been an evolution... a part of my life itself.

And, it has been a process and a season of self-discovery; of finding out who I was in Christ.

However, it was only once I was in compliance with His Word, in complete submission to Him, and following biblical scriptures and reference points, that I was able to realize an unspeakable peace, an unspeakable joy, and an unspeakable love for Christ I had never known before.

I believe that by sharing this testimony of my life's journey of self-discovery, the door will be opened for other men to do the same and to learn what I've learned... Such as, how to overcome fear and eliminate self-doubt, in order to become all that God had created them to be. And, being assured that, as God's sons, we are beautifully and wonderfully made, in the image of His firstborn son, Jesus Christ.

So, my prayer is that this will become more than just a book for you. I pray that it will become a movement; a template or roadmap you will use to allow the Holy Spirit to reach that place within you where *Extra-ordinary* lives.

A MAN AFTER GOD'S HEART

And when He had removed him, [God] raised up unto them David to be their king; to whom also He gave testimony, and said, "I have found David the son of Jesse, a man after mine own heart, which shall fulfil all my will.
~Acts 13:22

My parents divorced when I was very young, while I was in the second or third grade. Growing up in New Orleans, I remember experiencing two major hurricanes; Camille being the last one in August, 1969.

The next thing I remember is boarding a train with my brother, two sisters, and mom for the long ride from Louisiana to California.

When we arrived in California, life just started over. We moved in with my uncle, and as I look back now, I realize that I didn't really understand our family dynamic at the time. The only thing I knew was that I had my mom, my brother, and my two sisters.

However, I also knew that no matter where we were, or what was going on, daddy was going to show up. Therefore, nothing about my childhood seemed abnormal to me. Mom put us in school, I met other boys and girls, and life was good.

On Christmas Eve, my mom woke me up in the middle of the night, and my dad was standing there in the doorway. The overwhelming joy I had in seeing him caused me to immediately get out of the bed to jump into his arms.

I remember sensing such an amazing joy!

I will never forget how I felt, knowing my dad was with us in that moment.

Although they were divorced, my dad was always very close and continued to have a very strong presence in my life, even throughout my college years. I didn't know (or really care) how all of the legal stuff worked, I just knew I could always count on him being around. And for that, I was thankful.

My older brother, my older sister, and my younger sister and I, are all four years apart. When we relocated to California, my brother and sister were in their teens, and my younger sister was a toddler.

We each have different memories of childhood, and there were times I would become perplexed, witnessing my siblings struggle in their relationships with both of my parents; trying to understand the various feelings they would have.

There were many times throughout my adulthood, where I held frustration and anger toward some of my siblings. Having always viewed my mom as the rock, I could never understand how anyone would see her differently.

Growing up through the years, I never felt that I, nor my brother and sisters, lacked for anything; because, mom provided everything for us.

She was our foundation.

At a very early age, she was my inspiration... my *Shero*. Even though dad was near, Mom was the anchor, and everything revolved around her; becoming a vision for me of what motherhood, parenthood, and adulthood looked like.

My mom went back to school as a full-time mom, part-time student, and full-time worker. So, she was not only a vision of motherhood and adulthood, she was also my template of what hard work and success looked like.

Nevertheless, Mom wasn't one to complain, and as time went on, I began to learn more about her, as she would share bits and pieces of her upbringing with me during our conversations, as well as some of the pain she had experienced in life. Thus, allowing me to have a greater understanding of all that she had overcome.

My relationship with my dad was unique, and as I got older, it became stronger. I was able to put the pieces together and see the man he was and the struggles he had.

In his own way, he would become an amazing role model for me, as well.

As a young adult, when my dad and I would meet for coffee, dinner, or breakfast, he would always ask me before we left, "Son, is there anything you want to talk about?"

I would always answer, "No, daddy, I'm good. Everything is fine." He would say, "Are you sure? I'm not going to be around for long, so if there is something you want to talk about, we can talk about it right now."

I would repeatedly tell him that I was fine, and that I would see him next week. Looking back now, I miss those moments. I miss having the opportunity to sit and talk about life with him.

See, back then, I was too busy trying to conquer the world, and now when I talk to my 29-year-old son, Johnathan, I find myself having that same dialogue; "Is everything okay, son?"

He always responds like I did with my dad, "Dad, I'm fine."

My dad never finished high school, but when I was younger, he went back and got his GED. He made a decision to change the direction of his life.

I didn't know he was a recovering alcoholic at the time, but learning of the tough decisions and changes he had made in his life, only served to strengthen my admiration of him.

He wasn't a very a religious man, nor did he attend church all the time. My dad rarely spoke of God, but he would consistently speak of his faith and encourage me to pray.

When I look back at his life now, I'm so proud of him. After he received his GED, he joined the U.S. Postal Service and became a drug and alcohol counselor; an ironic turn of events in his life.

But God!

After retirement, my dad moved back to New Orleans to live close to his mom and his sister, so he could help take care of them.

Not long afterward, when we discovered that Daddy had been diagnosed with cancer, I would travel back and forth to check on him in New Orleans; spending time with him to help him get his affairs in order, because as he was getting sicker, I started having fears about the limited time we had left.

By the grace of God, through the years, my parents had been able to come to a place of peace with one another. I'm sure my mother knew that he still loved and cared for her; however, my dad honored and respected her new marriage. Art was now a vital part of the family, and my dad accepted that.

The dynamics of my parents' relationship had a profound impact on me, and both my mom and Art's acts of compassion and love toward my father, during his battle with cancer, still resonate with me today. Now that I have been divorced myself, I have learned that you can still be compassionate and demonstrate love for the other person.

In Pat Conroy's, "The Prince of Tides", there is a scene near the end when Tom goes back to his family. Reflecting on his life, he says, *"In families, there are no crimes beyond forgiveness."*

Watching the family issues and drama that occurred throughout that movie really resonated with my spirit and was an eye-opening experience for me; reminding me of the hardships my own family had been through. I firmly believe that no matter where we are in life, or what we go through, we, as a family, should always be there; willing to forgive one another's sins.

My last memory of my father was when he went to meet the Lord. My brother, Ben, had come down, and we were taking shifts watching over him.

It was early in the morning, around 2am, and Daddy was resting in bed. I think he knew Ben and I were with him, and it appeared he was in a good place.

Daddy's house in New Orleans was a single story, and there weren't any windows in the room he was staying in. Yet, my dad was looking at the wall to his left, as if he were peering out a window.

His gaze was fixed.

You could talk to him, but he would not turn his head to look at you; he just kept staring at the wall with a sense of peace on his face.

I remember asking him, "Daddy, what are you looking at?"

Silence.

I knew he was able to respond, because if we were to ask a completely different question, he would answer.

So, I continued to ask, "What do you see?"

He still wouldn't tell us.

I remember asking him, "Are you afraid of what you see?"

He shook his head. "No"

For 30 minutes, God had his complete attention, and my dad was conscious of it. He uttered a few inaudible whispers, as if having a private discourse with God, and I knew he was ready to go.

My brother and I told him that we loved him, and he just smiled, while looking out "the window".

Watching his transition changed my life.

God revealed Himself so strong in that moment, and I know that if I hadn't known God before, I would have known him then.

What a glorious and loving God He was.

I will never forget it; it was one of the most peaceful, and joyful experiences of my life. Most people would consider losing a parent a traumatic experience, but it was an amazing blessing to watch my dad, at the age of 63, move on to the next life with God; knowing that due to the changes he had made in his later years, he had accepted Christ as his Lord and Savior, and left the world in a much better place.

It wasn't a sermon, or a specific message, or sitting in a pew at church that strengthened my relationship with God - it was just me and my brother sitting on the side of the bed - watching God's love at work with my dad.

At my father's funeral, I found out that I had a sister I didn't even know existed. He had a daughter from an earlier relationship, before I was even born.

Once I had started to put the pieces together, I began to clearly understand how the dynamics of relationships and divorce within my family were passed down; recognizing that although my parents had gotten married to each other, they had been in previous relationships.

I didn't know it at the time, but growing up in a single-parent household did have an effect on us. Not having a model as to what a married family was supposed to look like contributed to my siblings and myself having all been married and divorced.

We just didn't have a Godly template for success.

My older sister has been divorced, and is remarried to a wonderful man, named Chris... My younger sister is divorced. My brother has been married and divorced. And, my mom is married to Art, whom I love to life, and they have been together now for 20 plus years.

I've been married and divorced twice.

Mom has shared with me a few times, that the third time is the charm.

You better believe I received that!

My dad, however, never remarried. He might have dated maybe once or twice, but I know that he never stopped loving my mom, and I know that he had many regrets; I'm sure, wishing he could have done things differently. I remember his longing spirit, and I believe before he went home to be with the Lord, he wished he would have had that soul-mate with whom to share the remaining years of his life.

Although neither of my parents' experiences were mine, I soon realized that once you understand someone's story, you can not only empathize with them, but also have love and compassion for them.

After this, I also began to see that each of my siblings had their own relationship with our parents, and accept the knowledge that you can live and grow up in the same house, yet have distinctly independent experiences and feelings towards life and one another.

I believe that as we mature and get older, we become more reflective. I'd like to believe I've become less judgmental, and more understanding and compassionate, as I reflect on the relationships within my family of origin and how we arrived at where we are today; thankful to God that everyone is in a safe or good place, and we are still growing.

It did take time to really be open and look at it like that, and to see how we all became who we are today, due to our relationships with each other.

Then, God wasn't first in my life. So, neither the reasons why I got married, nor the reasons why I got divorced, were Godly.

My son Jonathan is single, and he and I have a very transparent relationship; which I greatly treasure. It allows me to function as a role model for him, to share my life experiences with him, and to help him understand what a husband and a father should be in God's eyes.

It was a very important time in my life when I began to learn the Word of God. When God brings the right people into your life to teach you His Word, you will begin to become a better person.

Yes, knowledge is power!

Once you know the Word of God, you have no more excuses; however, you have to *want* to change. You need to be able to say, "God, I know I can't continue to live the way that I live."

I recognized I had been doing things my way and they hadn't worked out, so I needed to do something different; to admit that I needed God's help.

It was then I became empowered with the Word to make changes; not to become perfect, but to make effective changes to live the right way.

THE DAVID TEMPLATE

David is an excellent example of a man who shines forth and rises to God's preordained, predestined position, despite other's opinion of his value. In the eyes of most, especially his family, David's potential and purpose appears to have been overlooked, or at best, minimized.

He was the youngest of eight boys in his father's home. He was more than likely seen as "just" the baby... the runt. He was "just" the little Shepherd boy.

In fact, when Samuel the Priest arrived to anoint the next King, David was out in the field tending the sheep.

After examining the sons presented to him, Samuel asked Jesse, "Do you have any other sons?"

Only then, was David even considered.

A pivotal point is that even after David was anointed, he went right back to tending sheep. He did not boast or brag to his family of his pending position; he did not sit back and wait to be king; he walked in his place until his position was prepared.

Despite what his own family thought, David continued to excel; even in what seemed like the menial occupation of shepherd, his valor revealed itself as he killed both a lion and a bear.

One day while delivering food to his elder brothers, who were on the battlefield, David met a fierce Philistine warrior, by the name of Goliath. Although David had no foreknowledge of this impending confrontation, while others who were themselves mighty warriors, shuddered with fear, this young man of valor rose to the challenge that was issued.

Offered the heavy, fortified armor that was commonly worn in war, David chose to decline; because although it may have been appropriate for the occasion, it was ill-fitted for him the person. David used what was familiar to him - a sling and a few smooth stones; and with this, defeated a formidable opponent.

David continued to be a valiant warrior and went on to become the King of Israel.

David shows how one can come from humble beginnings; from a less than perfect family life; can be initially overlooked or underestimated - but can be elevated to great heights and do extraordinary things; simply by staying true to who you were created to be, and allowing GOD to position and prosper you at the proper time.

REFLECTION

What Chapters of Your Life Do You Need God to Help You Understand?

A FAITHFUL SPIRIT

And Pharaoh said unto his servants:
'Can we find such a one as this,
a man in whom the spirit of God is?'
~*Genesis 41:38*

I believe God always has something destined for each of us. However, after going to college for a couple of years, I bounced around in various jobs for another year and a half. I needed something to help my focus and change the present course of my life.

Back then, I was a young dad looking for stability in a career that would help provide for my family; not only for the moment, but also for the future. I always had a passion for aviation, loving airplanes and jets, and I had been in the Air Force JRROTC while in high school. So, I had a familiarity with the military, and knew that I would receive the stability I desired, while enlisted, as well as when I got out.

Therefore, I decided to enter the Service.

One early Saturday morning, I went to the recruiter's office, walked up the stairs to a co-located suite of sorts for all the branches, and knocked on the Air Force recruiters' door; however, no one was there.

As I'm knocking, the Army recruiter pipes up and asks, "Excuse me, can I help you?" I responded, "Yeah, where's the Air Force guy?"

I'll never forget his reply: "If I can guarantee you the career that you like, would you be willing to sign up with us?" I had no intention of joining the Army, but told him I'd take a look. He showed me various jobs within the aviation field, specifically ones working with helicopters, and was able to lock in a position for me on the spot.

The Air Force lost me because they went out for lunch, and I went into to the Army as a Blackhawk mechanic, UH-60 crew chief. As it turned out, the Army was the right way to go.

Truly, I believe to this day, that every young man should have the opportunity to be in the military for a minimum of two years. I think it should be a standard in our country that every man should serve their country in a military purpose.

It does several things for you, depending on the stage of life when you enter.

First, it provides you with a strong sense of maturity and responsibility, as well as discipline (even more-so if you weren't raised having that structure in your life).

Secondly, it gives you respect for the rights and privileges we have as citizens of the United States.

And I tell people all the time, just because you joined the military doesn't mean that you are going to go to war or fight, or that you are going to carry a weapon every day.

There are so many careers to choose from; so, take every opportunity and max out every benefit. Because, once you leave the military and transition into civilian life, you not only have those transferable skills gained in the Service, but also lifelong benefits: favorable financial assistance to purchase a home for the very first time, access to health care, retirement, etc.

I got out of the Army (active duty) in 1988, but followed it with two years of National Guard. Then, military life led right into my corporate experience, where I took my Blackhawk training to the civilian side, got my A&P (Airframe and Powerplant) license from the FAA, and began to work on airplanes.

In 1990, I was hired by a major airline to work on jets as an aircraft mechanic; going from being a Crew Chief in the military, to an aircraft mechanic role, as a civilian. I did everything from changing brakes and tires, to fixing tray tables in the inside cabin.

And I learned very quickly that I did not want to work on the outside of the plane, due to the rain and heat; therefore, I decided to learn how to work on avionics (the electrical portion) of the aircraft and moved inside right away, because of the skills I had acquired in the military.

I enjoyed avionics, not only because it was an inside job, but because it was a career with great pay and great benefits. It was an important role, well-respected by other people, and I was doing it so well that I was soon approached by my station manager, who was able to see some things in me that I couldn't see, to ask if there was an interest in going into management.

It was the furthest thing from my mind; especially working in a union environment. At the time, I was a union employee, quite young and impressionable, with a mindset that it was the employees against the management team.

So, I said, "No".

Nevertheless, his character drew me to the position, and within six months, he had convinced me to take a position as an entry-level supervisor on the midnight shift; leading a team of mechanics.

From there, I rapidly moved up the proverbial career ladder, ultimately, being promoted to Regional Manager; overseeing a staff of about 2500.

I was one of the first - and one of many - when we look back today at African Americans who were rising in aviation. However, when I look back over those years, it was pretty aggressive advancement... and I wasn't prepared for it. Not only from the perspective of experience, but also because I was still learning how to fly; both figuratively and spiritually.

See, although I understood that in life our priorities should be, God first, my young family second, and then career third, in reality, it wasn't.

In truth, it became career first and second, and then family bundled with church and everything else, last.

Work wasn't close to our home, with us living about 70 miles away from Los Angeles International (LAX). Therefore, I would drive 140 miles round-trip every day for work; leaving my house around 4 a.m. to get to the office by 5 a.m. for conference calls.

I would try to leave the office by 5 p.m. in order to beat traffic and get back home; arriving with just enough time to shower and give everybody a kiss on the cheek, before going to bed and starting the cycle all over again the next day.

I didn't have a healthy balance in my life.

While I was doing an exceptional job from a business standpoint, I was failing miserably at home.

This mindset originated from the belief that I was doing what I was "supposed to do" in my role as a dad and husband. As a young man, you are always taught that your primary responsibility is to provide for your family... by any means necessary; making it my excuse to not to spend time with the kids or with my wife, because I gave them a beautiful home and a nice car.

It didn't matter that I was rarely there.

Yet, while I was working so hard to keep everyone else happy, I had begun to lose myself; still searching to find out who I was.

As the African American Manager of a major airlines maintenance firm based in Los Angeles, I had become focused on titles and promotions.

This is why we must be careful when making decisions whether or not to accept promotions. It is important that we evaluate the opportunity to determine if we are truly prepared for them and to discern when it's God elevating you, or when man is elevating you.

Now don't get me wrong, I know God was with me the entire time. I just recognize the decisions made regarding my career, marriage, and family time, were my choices. And although I did well financially, my marriage and family suffered, because I was never home.

I didn't have a healthy understanding of what marriage was, what a family was, and most importantly, what I should be doing in my role to maintain it all.

During this time of realizing that something wasn't right, but not knowing what was missing, September 11th happened.

I remember that morning. I was at work early, preparing for conference calls, and someone ran into my office and said, "You know, Jim, we believe there has been an accident in New York; an airplane has just crashed into a building."

My initial thought was it was a small airplane and something random had happened. I turned on the TV in the conference room, but went back to getting prepared for my call. Within two short minutes, the lights on the office phones lit up -- everything just went red. I'll never forget that moment, because it changed my life dramatically.

If you can imagine, a major airport like LAX, has activity 24 hours a day. Yet, once it had been closed down and non-critical employees sent home, it quickly became a ghost town; empty and desolate.

The magnitude of what had unfolded was enormous, and for the first time, I understood how quickly things could change; how roles could be redefined in an instant, especially when you are depending on someone else to provide your sense of completeness with supposed income "security".

A month or two later, we had our first massive layoff at the station. The company had decided that a reduction in force was necessary. These were people I had "grown up" with, who worked hard, and had helped me in so many ways.

I'll never forget that feeling of despair; having to layoff so many people, and seeing how lives were impacted.

Then, I was let go, too.

The morning I was let go, I remember walking to my office like any other normal morning, and was met by corporate security. Another member of management from a sister-station already had boxes packed with my things, outside my door.

When you hear, *"hope everything works out for you Jim; take care of yourself"*, it shifts your life. I felt like, *My God, how could You? Oh my God, all these years!*

It caused me to stop and think about my life. My divorce wasn't final and I was involved in a new relationship. A sense of fear began to overwhelm me, as my role was taken from me, and I became uncertain about my future: *What am I going to do now? How am I going to live? How am I going to pay for things? How am I going to maintain these two homes?*

However, I wasn't out of work long. Within two weeks, I received a call for a Director of Aircraft Maintenance position for a small aviation company.

Without asking or seeking God, I went down for a quick interview, said "Yes" to the position, and relocated to Northern California.

I was at the new job for about a year. And then I felt a shift. Investors were in town reviewing the company, and we were taking them around for flights throughout the day, sightseeing, and looking at the airplanes.

It was the end of the day, a Friday, and I remember leaving to go home. It's a weekend and I knew that I would see everybody that following Monday. I hadn't been home for 15 minutes, when I had a call from the office.

An aircraft was missing; they've lost an aircraft.

"What do you mean they lost the aircraft?" The voice on the phone repeated the aircraft number and that it was gone. It was already dark, so no one could go out and search, but I drove back to the airport; staying for the rest of the night with others who had returned and the search teams.

I stayed at the airport; I didn't go out for the search and rescue. They found the airplane and the four souls who had lost their lives. In that moment I knew, God had spoken to me so clearly.

He had my full attention.

In that short night shift, I knew my aviation career was over. 9/11, the layoff, and now this... I could no longer run. I had to stop running.

Even though I knew Christ and I was a faithful servant who attended church and Bible study, and was head Usher and a part of the Deacon's board, I began to realize that those titles really had nothing to do with a relationship with Christ.

For the very first time, I just stopped and truly sought God about what was I going to do next. "What is it that You are calling me to do?"

After taking some time to really listen for the answer, it was clear to me that my innermost desire was to be a Professional Speaker. I believe that it is something that I do well, and I am making a greater impact serving God, than I was in my other positions.

I now know that I didn't have to take any man's offer of a role or promotion, nor accept Man's definition of success.

The Word says you should *seek His kingdom first*. That has become the true measure of success for me. It states it right there. When you seek His Kingdom first, everything else you need will come.

We tend to value ourselves based on how much money we have, but we have to learn that money is a resource; it's not who you are.

Your true level of success will be an outcome of your relationship with Christ. That's where I missed it; I sought man's validation, man's guidance, and man's template.

Now, as a Speaker, I have many God-fearing and anointed mentors and role models, in my life; however, I remember to seek God *FIRST*!

It's very dangerous to place your career and life choices in another man's hands.

It doesn't matter if it is your Manager, your business partner, your Pastor, or your Coach. When you are seeking out that person, when your relationship with that person is close to replacing what you should seek in a relationship with Christ, when that person becomes your god in a sense, you are modeling your life after that person.

For me, I had to make the transition from doing things to please man, to doing things to please God; No longer for the approval, the prominence, or the applause of Man. I don't need my name on the door of a corner office, or a high-level title on my business card. I just need to be the best Jim that I can be for Christ.

Where the last chapters of my life were for me, this Chapter is for God; using the gifts that He has given me, to expand the Kingdom, and for His Glory.

THE JOSEPH TEMPLATE

God set the standard through Joseph as a man dedicated to the discipline of holding firm to the promises of God despite the process required before the actual manifestation occurred.

The process is that undisclosed portion of the journey between when the promise is presented and perceived, and when the promise is actually fulfilled. The length of this process is usually as mysterious as each of the elements that comprise it, and is uniquely individual to each person.

Joseph endured many things in his process, any one of which singularly would have been devastating; but when combined, they created a chain of events that flipped his world completely upside-down.

From the moment he shared his dream with his brothers, and they began to plot against him, until the time they sold him into slavery; then him being seduced and falsely accused by his master's wife, which resulted in him being imprisoned as a result... even to the point of him being seemingly forgotten in that dungeon...the events of his process were daunting. Though faced with disappointment after disappointment, Joseph remained devoted to God and His promises.

GOD used the sum total of Joseph's experiences to fortify his faith; and his faith was the thing that sustained him until the process was completed and the promise became evident. Ultimately, because of the unique gift that God had instilled in him, Joseph was released, redeemed, and rewarded.

Not only was Joseph blessed, he became a tremendous blessing to his family, his people and to others.

Joseph's focus and unrelenting determination to hold fast to God's promises despite circumstances, can certainly serve as inspiration for anyone who has recognized the promise, but has not yet realized it's fulfillment.

REFLECTION

What Areas of Your Life Are You Putting Ahead of God?

FINDING A GOOD THING

He who finds a wife finds what is good
and receives favor from the Lord.
~Proverbs 18:22

When I married at 23, I wasn't prepared.

I married my first wife because she was a nice person, had a great career, and was attractive.

Having divorced her husband to marry me, I know that God didn't bring us together. We brought ourselves together, based on the desires of our flesh.

We didn't seek Him; we sought each other from a physical standpoint as we were trying to fill voids within ourselves.

We were married for almost 15 years. However, as I mentioned previously, I did not have a template of what a Godly marriage should look like. So, I did not fully understand what my role as a husband should be... much less my role as a father.

Therefore, the role I played in my marriage was based on what I thought the world said it should be.

Meaning, as a man, I went to work and provided for my family from a material standpoint.

That was my singular focus.

We also attended church as a family, but at the time, I didn't have a relationship with Christ. And, although I cannot say whether or not my (then) wife did, I do know that we didn't walk out the model of a Godly marriage.

Overall, I believe I did a pretty good job, yet the most important point is that I didn't seek God. He was in the periphery, and at that time in my life, His perspective, plan, and guidance were secondary.

It was this way not only throughout my first marriage, but my second as well, as I had re-married not more than 30 days after my divorce was finale. And again, God didn't bring us together.

We did.

Especially considering the fact that when I began dating my second wife, my first wife and I were only separated, not divorced; behavior that supported the fact that although I was looking for love, I instead was developing relationships through premarital sex and fleshly desires.

That was a recipe for disaster!

Brothers, if you select your partner based solely on how you feel, rather than on what God says, it's all flesh at that point. Premarital sex and creating ungodly soul ties are the death of a relationship.

Though the term "soul tie" is not used in the Bible, it refers to this concept when it mentions souls being "knit together", such as the friendship between a younger (soon to be King) David and Jonathon, the son of King Saul:

"And it came to pass, when he had made an end of speaking unto Saul, that the soul of Jonathan was knit with the soul of David, and Jonathan loved him as his own soul." ~ I Samuel 18:1

Where the previous example demonstrates a positive effect, there are both negative and positive effects of a soul tie. Pre-marital or extra-marital affairs can create soul ties that are not easily broken, due to the parties becoming one outside of a marriage covenant.

This is best described in the book of Genesis, *"When Shechem the son of Hamor the Hivite, prince of the country, saw her [Dinah], he took her, and lay with her, and defiled her."* ~ Genesis 34:2

Lust is more than strong sexual desire. When relationships are born out of lust, it means that it was founded upon an unrestrained need to please oneself through possession of another thing or person. There are several examples of this type of relationship in the Bible. Samson, who had Delilah, is one and David, who had Bathsheba, is another.

There was a price to pay for both!

If you have found yourself in this situation, my friend, let me give you some advice:

"Just say No."

A soul tie connotes a level of intimacy; a strong emotional attachment and sense of loyalty. The two souls are as one in the spirit. And, in its healthiest presentation, it is an inherent and beneficial component of a covenant marriage.

Needless to say, prior to both of my marriages, I had no concept of what it meant to operate in a covenant marriage.

I've since learned.

In his book, *"The Marriage You've Always Dreamed Of"* (2005), Dr. Greg Smalley, who is the Executive Director of Marriage and Family Formation at **Focus on the Family**, and the author of 40 books on marriage, shared that a covenant marriage is *"intended by God to be a lifelong fruitful relationship between a man and a woman. Marriage is a vow to God, to each other, our families and our community to remain steadfast in unconditional love, reconciliation and sexual purity, while purposefully growing in our covenant marriage relationship."*

With that knowledge, it is important to differentiate a "Covenant" from a "Contract".

They are not the same thing!

According to Merriam-Webster, the dictionary definition of a contract is: "A binding agreement between two or more persons or parties; especially one that is written and legally enforceable."

The interesting thing to note about contracts is that it requires all parties to 'hold up' or perform their end of the agreement. Should one (or both) of the parties neglect to do so, then this is considered a "breach" of contract; making it null and void.

The parties can simply walk away.

Nowhere in the Bible does God talk about entering into a 'contract' for marriage.

However, the word 'covenant' is one of the most frequently used words in the Bible; translated in Hebrew close to 300 times!

In the Old Testament, it is translated from the Hebrew *'Berîyth'* [Strong's\ #1285], derived from a root which means "to cut; both parties having a portion of the whole.

Therefore, a covenant marriage is "a coming together" of the two parts... a joining, a cleaving... a bond, much like Super Glue! This is why the Word of God states in both the Old and New Testament, *"For this cause shall a man leave his father and mother, and shall be joined [cleave or bond] unto his wife, and they two shall be one flesh."*

So when I am now able to look at what the template of a Godly relationship or a Godly marriage looks like, it is this sacred covenant.

It is not meant to be broken!

Nevertheless, in both of my marriages, I did not realize my wives' needs from a Biblical standpoint. Therefore, whenever we struggled, we had nowhere to go; instead, attempting to resolve issues and figure out solutions to our problems, the world's way. Such as, meeting a brother over a drink to discuss things, or maybe she would connect with close friends or family for advice. Still, neither of us seeking God, or even godly counsel, for help.

We were not knit together as one.

Reflecting on life, I can now look back and say that I was married to two truly wonderful women. They were just two truly wonderful women that God didn't bring into my life for the purpose of marriage.

Not having had a comprehension of the meaning of the word covenant or the sacred meaning of marriage itself, I was not aware of the tremendous difference between the world's view of marriage and a Godly marriage.

The world's concept of marriage is extremely self-focused and self-centered. It's a simple thing to get married and divorced in our society. We get married based on our emotional, physical, financial, or material needs; if it doesn't work out, we just discard it and effortlessly move on.

However, The Bible instructs husbands to love their wives as Christ loves the church. We are to give ourselves up for her, as He did, by loving her, feeding her, caring for her; even as we would ourselves.

This is not a selfish love at all.

A man is to honor his wife. I didn't honor my wives as God desired me to. I provided, loved and gave material things. Yet, God requires so much more at a deeper level, and the Word teaches us—commands us—to honor our wife.

I know someone is saying right now, *"Man, you have no idea how my wife acted, or what she did."*

You're right, I don't.

Even so, I do know two wrongs don't make it right! It takes three people for a marriage to work. God, you, and your spouse!

"...a threefold cord is not quickly broken."
~Ecclesiastes 4:12b

It's important as men that as we honor our wives; that we don't objectify them and no, we can't place them on a pedestal. We must love our wives as truly and as much as Christ loves the church. And, if you don't have that relationship with Christ, if you don't have that Biblical template for your marriage, then you don't have the foundation for a strong covenant.

Christ has to be the centerpiece of your marriage. He needs to be the beginning, center, and end – the Alpha and Omega. You and your spouse must love and honor Him together.

The Bible is now my instruction book and I understand that you cannot embrace a sacred covenant of marriage based on a physical or an emotional need. Nor is it something to enter into lightly. If you don't know who you are or whose you are in Christ, you are setting yourself and your spouse (and ultimately your family), up to fail.

We as men love a challenge and believe we can fix everything. But truly, if you are not walking into your marriage together with godly counsel, seeking

God first, and knowing He brought you together, no matter what you do, you will struggle.

Only Christ can fill the role as your first love.

THE BOAZ TEMPLATE

Boaz models for us an excellent example of a godly man who demonstrates how to recognize, and properly pursue, protect, and provide for his wife.

Note that Boaz was himself well established in certain key areas, before he even inquired about Ruth; let alone pursued her...

First, he was established in his relationship with God. Out of his love for God, he developed obedience for God's laws. This in turn set in motion a chain of events that brought Ruth into his fields (Leviticus 19:9-10).

Then he was established as a man of means. He owned land, on which he grew crops; he had workers who harvested these crops, which provided for him and others. Thus, he was prepared to provide for his future wife. This was in place well before he inquired about Ruth.

Next, there was the process of pursuing Ruth. Boaz observed, and inquired, before he pursued her.

He took the time and effort to familiarize himself with who she was, and also of her circumstances and history. Having a foreknowledge of this allowed him to better prepare himself to care for her. Yes, he was attracted to her physically; but because he had learned enough about her, he was equally attracted to her inner qualities.

The impressive thing about Boaz is that he did all of these things before he married her. He proved himself to be a capable priest, provider and protector, before he ever became her kinsman redeemer and husband.

He acquired for her, the land of her deceased husband, and in so doing, honored her family; then he married her.

REFLECTION

In What Ways Can You Demonstrate that You are Willing to Love Your Wife as Christ Loved the Church?

LEAVING A LEGACY

A good man leaveth an inheritance
to his children's children
~Proverbs 13:22a

My role as a father has grown over the years into multiple layers. However, going back to that original idea of what it was, I had a truly unique model in the investment of both of my parents; in spite of their divorce.

Although my dad did a wonderful job in helping to raise me, my Mother was my foundation. She instilled structure, discipline, responsibility, and love into my life.

I've already detailed my father's successful accomplishments later in life and the positive mark he left upon me. So, let me take a moment to share with you a little about my Mother, who was my role model and as far back as I can remember, always progressive and ahead of her time.

As a young child in the late 60's, she was just "Momma". Yet, she owned and operated her own Nursery/Daycare Facility. I can still recall being there with her throughout the day, and after all the other children had gone home, sneaking back into the kitchen to take a few cookies from the giant glass cookie jar in the cabinet.

(I was just being a boy Mom.)

I can only imagine the many thoughts that went through her mind, as she boarded that train to Los Angeles with four kids to start a new life.

While working full time and functioning as a single parent, she went back to college to finish her degree; soon becoming a beacon of hope and a trailblazer for women in the Transportation Industry, beginning her career at what was then called Southern California (RTD).

As the first female bus operator post-World War II, my mom became the first female in the history of the Authority in the following positions:

- Division Dispatcher
- Assistant Division Transportation Manager,
- Division Manager
- Transportation Superintendent
- and Director of Transportation

Then, after retiring in Los Angeles, she later became the Assistant General Manager of Operations for the City of Cleveland, Ohio.

Mother ended her transportation career in the city of New Orleans, as the Deputy General Manager of Operations.

You may ask, *"Why would you list each of your mom's transportation achievements?*

I do so, because it speaks to her legacy, and that's just in her professional career. I also do so, because it speaks to having an impact in the lives of your family and others, as well as the importance of we, as parents (especially Fathers) to lead by example... to help build the foundation of love, character, integrity, and responsibility into our children.

My parents were wonderful examples in my life!

However, when I became a father, I felt that being a good dad meant to simply make sure my son had everything he needed.

That was all, and that should be enough.

The understanding that a father needed to be fully present or to personally instill healthy values into that child's life—to help that child because a child doesn't have a choice—was absent, both in my way of thinking and in the application of what I thought I knew.

The primary goal to raise my child to be an effective citizen, while working to develop and sustain that relationship in order to support their ability to have a positive impact on the world itself, was not yet a priority. I wasn't at that stage in my growth as a man or a father.

Throughout my first marriage, my working belief was that a dad went to work, and when he came home at the end of the day, maybe he saw the kids for a little bit. There usually was an understanding by the father with the mother and she would let the kids know to leave dad alone. Saying, *"Your Dad's been working all day. He's got to get some rest."* Or, *"Give Daddy a kiss and you will see him tomorrow."*

Jonathan was about to turn 17 when I got divorced in my first marriage, and in my mind, I thought he was going to be just fine; this was his last year of high school and he was a good kid. I believed that we had done a pretty good job of raising him, so I went on with my life and my new marriage, not understanding that just because a child is "of age" doesn't mean that they are ready or prepared to take on the world and life itself.

It took me a long time to realize that I thought Jonathan was okay based solely on his age. I didn't become aware until later that he needed something more than dad writing him a check or showing up to a football game.

Yes, those things were important, but what he needed even more, was for me to *be* his Dad.

As parents, we have a soul tie with our children. This bond can be easily broken through divorce or by any act of separation from their life. If you don't have consistent active engagement and authentic expressions of love, while making sure your child feels secure in that love, beyond material things or physical possessions, both you and your child will miss out on a great gift!

As Fathers, it is our responsibility to build a strong foundation for our families. This is an exceptional privilege given to us by God Himself, who is also our Heavenly Father.

To neglect this role is of great consequence.

Though contemporary societal norms allow for us to bear children outside of marriage, God's standard is, and always has been, that becoming a father should occur after first being a husband.

"But since sexual immorality is occurring, each man should have sexual relations with his own wife, and each woman with her own husband. The husband should fulfill his marital duty to his wife, and likewise the wife to her husband. The wife does not have authority over her own body but yields it to her husband. In the same way, the husband does not have authority over his own body but yields it to his wife. Do not deprive each other except perhaps by mutual consent and for a time, so that you may devote yourselves to prayer. Then come together again so that Satan will not tempt you because of your lack of self-control. I say this as a concession, not as a command." ~I Cor. 7:1-5

For this reason, you'll notice, I discussed covenant marriage in the previous chapter, prior to discussing becoming a father. I now know that one must be prepared to be a good father. This doesn't happen just because a woman gives birth to our children.

Thankfully, we have the Word of God to help.

In the first part of Ephesians 6:4, the Apostle Paul instructs fathers not to *"provoke your children to wrath"*.

This doesn't mean not to properly discipline or set appropriate boundaries; however, it does mean not to intentionally do those things which will make our children become discouraged, resentful, or bitter. A godly father does not make up strict rules just to demonstrate that he is 'in charge' or exact unnecessary punishments in order to embed a sense of fear or dominance in their children.

Nor, does he remain absent in their child's life; whether he lives in the same house or not.

In the second part of that same verse, it states, *"but bring them up in the training and admonition of the Lord"*.

As the spiritual head of the home, a godly man gets the opportunity to imitate God, as a Father;

representing Him to his children. His loving presence in the lives of his sons and daughters should be felt through his teaching, leadership, and example.

However, when I first became a father, I wasn't a spiritual man. Not only was I not on the right path, I didn't have the proper roadmap or template from which to operate.

I know at times, we as men get lost in doing fatherhood the world's way. There's a belief that if I have a son, I need to show him I'm tough, that he has to be a man, and make sure there's no crying by telling him to "Man Up." By doing this, we miss opportunities to teach our sons how to respect themselves and to respect women.

Like our parents, we did the best we could with what we knew at the time; instilling those values in our children based on those values instilled in us— good and bad. But in that cycle, we continue to pass our mis-understanding from one generation to the next, imparting those negative aspects of fatherhood to our children as well.

Most recently, Jonathan lived with me in Houston for about two years. In that process of living with one another again, we had to reconnect and grow together, because I had no idea that there was such a gap in our relationship. I didn't know how much he was lacking and missing as a young man, due to my role as a long distance dad.

And that gap wasn't from a material standpoint; it was the things I should have been doing to help support his becoming a young man. Questions he needed answered, such as: What does it mean to love? Why do I need to have structure and discipline in my life? Or, just being available for him to say, *"Dad, I'm struggling with some things".*

And while I have one natural son, I also have three other step-children, Kemya and Jade (from my first wife) and Brittany (my second wife's daughter). I have been blessed to raise a family at a young age; and as they grew... I have also grown.

For me, the importance of fatherhood is now having a more cognizant present role in the family, while focusing more on being nurturing, as well as loving; *"Raising"* more than simply *"Providing"* the material side.

We have to use God's template and His template for father's is that *a good man leaves an inheritance*; not only for his first generation of offspring, but even to his children's children. This means that the fruit of the seed sown into the lives of his sons and daughters should continue to bear forth fruit into the next generation.

Another word used for inheritance is "legacy", which is defined in the dictionary as a gift handed down or endowed from one person to another.

Although leaving a legacy for our children may include a financial inheritance, such as houses, cars, land, or a high- yielding bank account, it goes well beyond that.

As godly fathers, the legacy we leave to our children must be that of great value. Something that, according to Proverbs 22:6, when they have grown old, they will not depart from, but pass down to their children... and generations to follow.

THE ABRAHAM TEMPLATE

Abraham, known as "The Father of Many Nations," is an exemplary portrait of fatherhood. Not that he was a perfect man, or a faultless father, but because he left a great legacy for many generations after him to follow.

As a man, Abraham teaches us the importance of faithfully obeying God, even when that obedience requires us to leave all that is familiar, safe and secure, and venture into the unknown. God simply told him to go, and He would show him where.

He took his wife Sarah, his nephew Lot, and his possessions, and did so; knowing only the promises of God:

1. That God would make his name great. Causing him to not only be blessed, but also to be a blessing.
2. That God would make him the Father of many Nations... even when he and Sarah had no children.

Abraham teaches us that in order to procure the Lord's promises, one must be willing to participate in the process; which may sometimes appear to be ill-timed, difficult, and lengthy.

Note that Abraham was not a young man when these promises were presented. Whether it was impatience or disbelief, something caused him to veer from the plan and take matters into his own hands; thus perhaps his first mistake as a father.

Following Sarah's suggestion, he married, and fathered a son (Ishmael) with Hagar; which created its own set of issues.

Abraham and Sarah eventually produced not one, but two sons - Isaac and Jacob (later named Israel, through whose family-line Jesus came).

Although Abraham accumulated massive wealth, and his sons acquired land and riches, it was his demonstration of faith in God which was his ultimate legacy.

REFLECTION

What Legacy are You Leaving for Your family?

_____
_____
_____
_____
_____
_____
_____
_____
_____
_____
_____
_____
_____
_____
_____
_____
_____
_____
_____
_____
_____
_____

AN ORDINARY MAN

As Jesus was walking beside the Sea of Galilee,
He saw Simon and his brother Andrew. They
were casting a net into the sea, for they were
fishermen. "Come, follow Me, Jesus said, "and I
will make you fishers of men." And at once they
left their nets and followed Him...
~ Matthew 4:18-20; Mark 1:16-18

Now in my 50's, I look back over my life and
survey the path I've walked as I've made my way to
Today. As a son, a husband, a father, and a young
man growing into the image of who God created me
to be, I saw the struggle...

Who am I?

Who am I supposed to be?

Who do I model my life after?

What does the world say a successful man is?

And, I know this wasn't just my struggle. As
men, most of us do, because we do not have godly
templates from which to pattern our lives. So

instead, we fumble our way around, like a car riding in the dark without headlights, believing that we know the road home.

Now, don't get me wrong. Many of us make a good show of it all. Much like when I was able to professionally navigate my way through military service and then a career in management. To anyone on the outside looking in, I was a man who had accomplished something great. Add in a smart, beautiful wife, a few kids, the white picket fence, and a couple of dollars in the bank, then stir.

Success... right?

Before answering that question, let's consider that moment spoken of in Matthew 4:19 and Mark 1:17, when Simon Peter and his brother Andrew were fishing along the Sea of Galilee.

Let's be clear about this. Peter and Andrew were not just fishing, nor were they simply laboring as fishermen. These brothers were productive businessmen in the city of Capernaum, the largest of the 30 fishing towns surrounding the sea, which was just beyond the Jordan. In other words, they had a trade and they were successful working their trade according to the blueprint they knew.

And then something happened!

They were approached by someone who had a different plan... a different perspective... a different purpose for their lives,

"And He saith unto them, Follow me,
and I will make you fishers of men."

In other words, I'm going to rearrange, redirect, and refocus what you are doing and transform it!

Right after this, Jesus comes across James and John mending their nets and called to them as well.

Now, these four men (who were the first of the twelve Disciples selected) did not just happen to meet Jesus in that moment; they were already aware of who He was, since He had been preaching in the area. Therefore, their decision to immediately lay down their nets and follow Christ was not due to their being in a foolish or hypnotic state.

Not at all! Having watched and listened to Jesus' teaching, they knew what type of man He was and were certain that by following Him, their lives would be changed for the better.

In much the same way I decided to follow my previous boss into management, the original twelve Disciples recognized a template they could pattern their lives after... and so they did; forever changing the course of not only their lives, but others as well.

Now, when I think of Jesus as that template, I recognize that He was the ultimate Servant Leader; He understood His purpose, which was *to serve God.*

He is the roadmap, and He is the model for our lives in the spirit of service. Jesus was always loving and compassionate, as He was there to serve. He was there to love; never judgmental, but taught God's work.

Jesus was a man of character, a man of ethics. He showed us God's purpose for our lives, and lived that purpose: one of service, one of love, one of peace, one of kindness, and one of joy.

Christ's sole purpose was to live and preach the Word of God. To that end, He taught. He gathered. He loved. He served.

Once you comprehend that your true purpose is also to serve, you too will *"immediately drop your nets and follow Him!"*

Unfortunately, many times we get completely lost in the labels we define ourselves with. Our jobs and careers have importance; however, we must remember that they are a gift God has given us. It's not enough for you to be doing whatever it is you are gifted, educated, or successful in, if what you are doing doesn't have God's purpose infused in it.

Instead, we make excuses. *Once I get to a certain level, I will truly be happy. It's a rough time at home, but if I can get this promotion, then everything is going to be okay. If I can make this much money, things will be great for us. I know I'm gone all the time, but it's how I can get our material things for happiness and joy.*

The truth is that no matter how much money you make, how many cars you buy, how many homes you have, how many women you've conquered, none of it will ever fill the void you have or answer the questions you're struggling with about your identity and purpose in life.

"The poorest person in the world is not the one without a single coin in his hand, but the one without GOD in his heart."

It wasn't enough for Peter, Andrew, John, and James to just be successful fishermen, if what they were doing wasn't in service to God or impacting the Kingdom for His glory.

Likewise, Christ shows us the perfect template after which we should model ourselves. When we are looking for that role model, guide, or mentor, He is that One.

See, even when I thought I had a measure of success, at the end of the day, I had to realize that I am going to be completely frustrated as long as I am not truly being who God created me to be. So, by recognizing that it's not about trying to become someone God didn't create, I could then become all that Christ has created within me.

Therefore, as I continue to move through the chapters and challenges of my life, it is important that I remember this point... this hard-earned lesson.

Thankfully, you don't have to waste all the time that I did. You don't have to waste all those years trying to navigate a roadmap of life. God has already given us the roadmap in the Bible. He's already given us that true North we are to follow—that compass is Jesus.

Today, when I look at the wonderful mentors and leaders I admire, they are men and women who took up the mantle, in order to become 'fishers of men'.

For me, this is what has become the ultimate template for my life. Despite the fact that it is an ongoing journey each and every day, I choose to follow Christ; the living template.

God gives us free will and He says you can go North or you can go South. He leaves the decision for us to make. However, He's already instilled the perfect compass within us—Christ is already in you.

If you follow His word, you can just walk it out.

I know I'm making it sound so simple, but if you truly wake up each and every morning saying, *"Okay, Father, how can I serve you today and what is it that You would have for me to do this day?"* you will hear, "It's to love, to serve, and to reach others for the Kingdom!

Once I knew and accepted the reality that I didn't have to be anyone else or live a life patterned after the World's Blueprint, I ceased searching! I didn't need to go to the next seminar, nor read anyone else's memoir or biography, to follow their template. If I read about a great person, who had lived what I would consider a successful life, it always led me back to God's Word and the living examples of Jesus.

Man will disappoint you. We elevate other people by placing them on a pedestal as our role models. We do it every day with our Sports figures, Pastors, Political leaders, and Celebrities. We lift them up and aspire to be like them.

Sooner or later, they fall short, causing us to be devastated, losing faith and hope, asking *"How could they have done that?"*

Not so in Christ.

Jesus will never disappoint you. He will never abandon you. He will never leave you in a place of disappointment. He will never break your heart.

We spend so much of our time looking for validation and esteem from Man. We want Man's approval that we are worthy; that we have done a great job and are ready for the next level.

Yet, only God can do that.

God elevates us. God promotes us. God opens doors. God gives us favor. Don't choose the path of doing it your way to attain success.

It will only leave you empty and unfulfilled.

In the Greek language, the word for disciple is *mathetes*. It means to accept and follow the views and practices of a teacher. This is what Peter, Andrew, John, James, and the other eight Disciples did, once called by Jesus.

They accepted that they had been living an ordinary life... as ordinary men.

However, once they chose to drop their nets and follow Him, to learn His will and His way, their lives began to become *extra-ordinary*.

In my life, I've decided to do the same.

JESUS CHRIST: THE PERFECT TEMPLATE

Of all those we might look to as a template to pattern our lives after, 1 Peter 2:21 points us directly to Jesus Christ as our perfect example. It does not matter which area of our life we may feel lacking, or in need of guidance, Jesus Christ is our ultimate answer.

I specifically point to Christ, because He is the representative within the Trinity who shines forth as God in the flesh. He is the one with whom we can readily relate, because there is absolutely nothing we have gone through, or will ever face, that he has not already experienced; and become victorious over.

Jesus has far too many positive attributes for us to cover, but there is one component which is key to all that He was able to accomplish - *His relationship with the Father*; and the knowledge that although he is Himself God, any earthly success he would appreciate, was contingent on his obedience to the Father.

The Christ shows us that once we embrace our eternal origin, it does not matter whether our life begins humble or grand; it does not matter how well-versed our networking skills, or how charismatic our personality - what determines our success is whether or not we are in a right relationship with God.

Yes, if we follow Christ's example, we learn to develop His character of love, patience, forgiveness, longsuffering, faithfulness, courage, strength, obedience and sacrifice; which is far more valuable than any natural or man-honored skills we can develop. In fact, godly character teaches us how to use these 'skills' to bring God glory.

As we continue to mature in Christ, He will reveal our true purpose and Destiny; place us on our path, and go before us to light the way.

"By humility and the fear of the Lord, are riches, and honour, and life." ~Proverbs 22:4

REFLECTION

What Changes do You Need to Make in order to Become Extra-ordinary ?

AN EXTRAORDINARY GOD

Now when they saw the boldness
of Peter and John, and perceived that they were
unlearned and ignorant men, they marveled; and
they took knowledge of them, that they had been
with Jesus.
~Acts 4:13

Just as Jesus called to each of His 12 Disciples, He is still calling ordinary men to follow Him, to learn of Him, and to re-present His character, His spirit, and His heart of service in the World today.

The people referred to in the book of Acts marveled at the change in Peter and John, not because of anything great or wonderful that they had done on their own, but because they recognized that these men "had been with Jesus."

And, much like the Apostles who had spent so much time eating, sleeping, and ministering to others with the Lord, we too can become bold witnesses of His extraordinary power in our lives.

However, you can only receive this ability to be transformed from ordinary to extraordinary once you are in relationship with Him; realizing that you cannot live this thing called life without Him.

For an ordinary man to understand his relationship with the Lord, it requires a strong sense of submission. Initially, it's going to feel awkward. It's going to feel uncomfortable.

It might even feel a bit painful.

Why? Because as men, we're used to being in control; making things happen on our own and in our own strength.

So in the natural, in your human flesh, you have to submit yourself. You have to die to the desires of your flesh and rely on Him. You must give your all to Him and say, *"Father, I can't do this without you. I need you to help me right now to be patient. I need you to remove this spirit of anxiety. I need you to remove this spirit of fear, the spirit of worry."*

Whatever your need is, submit it to Him... and then follow Him.

Trust in the Lord with all thine heart; and lean not unto thine own understanding. In all thy ways acknowledge him, and he shall direct thy paths.

~Proverbs 3:5-6

Of course, like all other relationships, it is one that takes work. When you don't feel like praying, pray anyway. When you don't understand what's happening, become quiet and listen, in order to hear His voice. When you're preparing to make a decision for your (or your family's) life, ask for His guidance and direction.

Let Him take the lead.

These are intentional acts of submission; it is you reaching out to Him and saying, *"Father, I need you more than anything else right now to help me to learn of you and to grow."*

He is constantly training, teaching, and speaking to us in every interaction we have. Each transaction or engagement with others should include Him and exhibit His character and His Word.

As you build your personal relationship with our Father, He replaces the unknown with certainty, fear with peace, and weakness with strength.

It's like Paul said:

> *"I can do all things through Christ who strengthens me."* ~Philippians 4:13

However, arriving at this level of submission doesn't happen overnight. It is a process of maturation, which takes time.

The Disciples may have followed Christ upon hearing Him call their names, but it took the next three and a half years of walking with Him for them to become the Apostles.

Remember Simon Peter?

Not only was he impulsive and strong-willed, he could in one moment make a profound and wise statement, but in the next minute be ready to cut off someone's ear! He was also one who denied knowing Jesus 3 times before the rooster crowed, because he was afraid that he would be killed as well.

However, during the day of Pentecost, after the Holy Ghost appeared, Peter was the first one to stand and testify of how extraordinary our God is.

This is exactly what He has done in my life.

Where I previously attempted to accomplish everything through my own knowledge and strength, today I look to Him for my direction and wisdom. My past was good, but with God, He has made my present and future great.

No... He has made it extraordinary!

As a man, I no longer seek love and validation from others, because I know that I am loved and validated by Him. The relationship I have with Him has secured me and empowered me to accomplish greater things with Him, than I ever could alone.

Believe me when I say, that as a professional mentor and trainer, I am aware it isn't that I'm an exceptional speaker, it's just that now God is using me to bless people in a way that it is evident I am in relationship with Him; that I have been with Jesus.

God is extraordinary. Once we realize this, we can rest, knowing that He already has everything under control and there is nothing we cannot overcome with Him. We can rely on Him, submit ourselves to Him, give our problems to Him, and watch Him work.

We decrease and allow Him to increase Himself within us. It doesn't matter what you do for a living, how much money you make, or where you went (or did not go) to school. Your particular profession or status in the world doesn't make a difference.

It is your heart of submission He wants.

You are an ordinary man who serves an extraordinary God. In each and every position He has placed you in, He wants you to become the man that He created you to be.

Whatever you are, as He created you, people should see Him. Wherever you are, you have a responsibility to do the work He has placed before you, with excellence. Understand that you are beautifully and wonderfully made through Christ and God has uniquely created you to serve your specific purpose on this Earth. He wants you to love like Christ loved; to serve like Christ served.

Yes, Christ is the perfect template. He came down from the royal throne room and though He professionally was a Carpenter, He was the most influential Carpenter the world has ever known.

He knew who He was and who He served and what His purpose was. He knew that He could serve exactly where He was, and in the same way, we can serve exactly where we are.

My life began when I walked to God's arms. When I called out to Him, He answered me. And, once I understood that all I needed to do was just be myself and serve others through Him, I discovered that I could do extraordinary things for people.

He has now added His *Extra* to my ordinary!

I have only been able to get through the previous chapters of my life by the grace of God. I just needed to position myself to receive His miraculous plan for the chapters to come.

He is calling you too.

In the midst of trial, in the midst of darkness, in the midst of confusion, and in the midst of doubt, you can start over.

It doesn't matter where you've come from or where you are now. God has created something perfect for you. You only have to receive it.

Trust Him, love Him, and walk with Him each and every day. He's walking along with you through each step of your journey.

Your life is just beginning.

The life of an ordinary man.

...with an extraordinary God.

YOUR NEXT STEP

Salvation cannot be earned... it is a Gift, freely given by God to all who ask for it. Romans chapter 10 states that, "if thou shalt confess with thy mouth the Lord Jesus, and shalt believe in thine heart that God hath raised him from the dead, thou shalt be saved...

For with the heart man believeth
unto righteousness; and with the mouth
confession is made unto salvation."

Romans 10:9-10

Now is the time. Say this prayer out loud:

"Dear Jesus, I believe that You are God and that You died for my sin, was raised from the dead, and are now alive, and hear my prayer. Therefore, I repent of all my sins and ask that You forgive me and come into my life as my Lord and Savior.

Teach me Your way and show me Your purpose for my life, that I may now live it in a way that pleases You.

Thank you for loving and saving me.

In Your Holy Name I pray... Amen!

Welcome to the beginning of an *Extraordinary* life!

"[For] I am crucified with Christ: nevertheless I live; yet not I, but Christ liveth in me: and the life which I now live in the flesh I live by the faith of the Son of God, who loved me, and gave himself for me."

~Galatians 2:20

To contact the author:

Email: Spknpro@Jimenezbailey.com

Website: JimenezBailey.com

Phone: 1-888-565-3318

DHBonner Virtual Solutions LLC
Editing | Author Coaching
www.dhbonner.net

KPE Media
Cover and Interior Design | Promotions
www.kpemedia.com?

Made in the USA
Monee, IL
31 January 2022

89483645R00066